# WHAT SHOULD
# I WEAR NOW?

Jana Sedláčková
Alexandra Májová

Albatros

long evening gown

fine-woven scarf

black turtleneck

dinner jacket with dress shirt, bow tie, and handkerchief

fur

tutu

dinner suit pants

cocktail dress

wraparound top with bow

patent-leather shoes

purse

stockings

dress shoes

necklace

opera glasses

bracelet

tickets

sports dress

pleated sports skirt

sports bra

tennis romper

sports headband

zip-up top and sports skirt

three-quarter-length pants

baseball cap

tennis shirt

short vest

wrist sweatbands

white tracksuit top

sun visor hat

tennis ball

white sports socks

sports shirt

baggy white shorts

racket

tennis shoes

flower headband

veil

colorful bowtie

colorful socks

jacket with buttonhole, vest, and shirt

wedding dress

petticoat

long gloves

lace shrug

necklace, bracelet, and earrings

dress pants

wedding cake

wedding dress shoes

rings

wedding bouquet

dress shoes

leather jacket

necklace

blouse with gathered sleeves

stylish T-shirt

casual shirt

bow wrap jumpsuit

frilly silk top

feathered earrings

moccasins

pants with creases

shirt-style dress with embroidery

denim jacket

dark pants

elegant sunglasses

black velvet dress shoes

flat gold shoes

flat purple shoes

handbag

watch

headscarf

eye mask with parrot feathers

party hat

fox mask

Viking set

witch's pointed hat

dinosaur costume

bee costume

old broom

witch costume

raccoon mask

skeleton suit

pirate hat

musketeer's hat

confetti

eyepatch

fan

princess's crown

moustache on a stick

ladybug costume

heart-shaped glasses

cat's-ears headband

soccer jersey

light sports jacket

tracksuit

boxer shorts with soccer pattern

soccer shorts

training socks

tank tops for each team

cleats

beanie

soccer jersey

soccer ball

yellow and red cards

shin guards

sports headband

referee's whistle

goalie gloves

long socks

sweatbands

captain's armband

training kit (jersey, shorts, socks)

school jacket

sleeveless sweater

hairband with bow

colorful shoes

baseball jacket

white shirt and bowtie

white shirt and tie

dress with flowery skirt

dinosaur T-shirt

plaid skirt

shorts with crease

triangle

school backpack

exercise books

jeans

long black socks

ballerina class shoes

long socks

break-time snack

scissors

pen

dress shoes

schoolbooks

map pencils

tennis shoes

nightcap

pajama top and shorts

lace nightdress

satin dressing gown

pajama top and long bottoms

three-quarter-length pajamas

slippers with bows

pillow

sleeping shirt with owl design

sleep mask

teddy bear

onesie with ears

slippers

straw hat

cowboy hat

leather jacket with tassels

bandana

overalls

plaid shirt

suspenders

cowboy boots

plaid blouse

warm jacket with wool lining

Plaid dress with ruffles

chaps with tassels

wool socks

wheelbarrow

rain boots

bucket

work gloves

pitchfork

Hang on while I pour out the rain from my sleeve . . .
I don't mind rain at all when I get to see a rainbow!
Hike
Funny umbrella he's using!
Oh dear. That artist's smock is getting soaked by the rain.
There must be better clothes to wear on a hike . . .

beanie

brim hat

baseball cap

cotton T-shirt

softshell jacket

raincoat

neck warmer

hiking shoes

convertible pants with zippers

sweatshirt

hiking socks

trekking poles

flashlight

backpack

camera

map

walking sandals

tank top

sunglasses

hiking boots

multi-tool

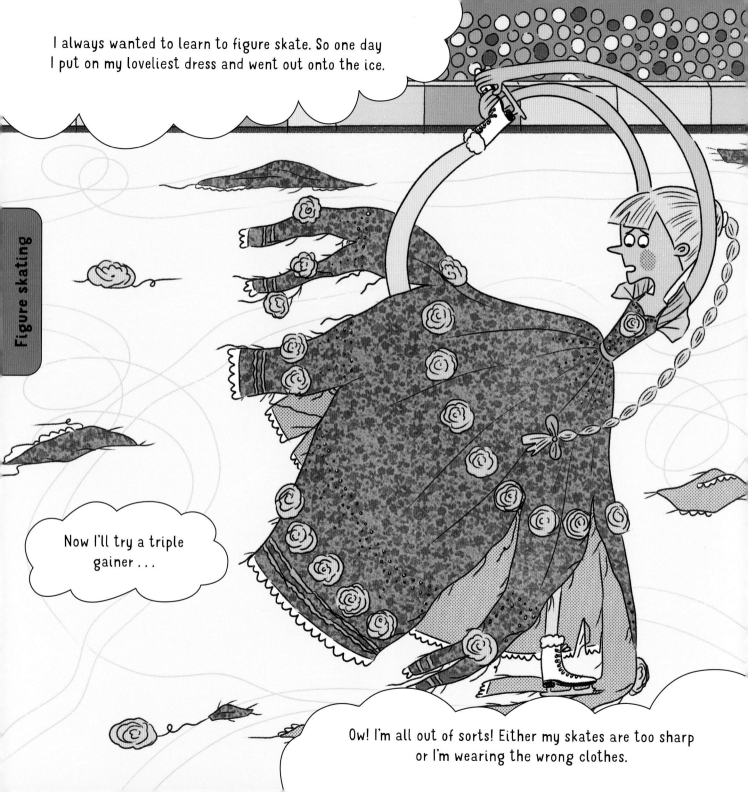

figure skater's leotard

competition dress with long sleeves

competition dress

competition dress with feather-effect skirt

leg warmers

hair accessories

ice skates

skater's tights

gloves

turtleneck

tank top

padded crash pants

warm headband

sports skirt

knee protectors

elbow protectors

figure skating suit

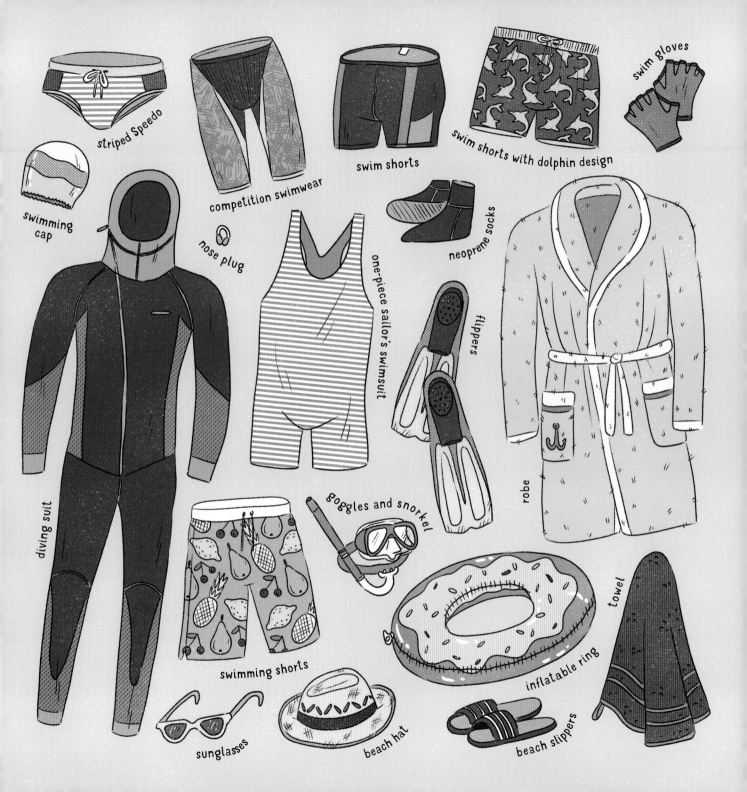

striped Speedo

competition swimwear

swim shorts

swim shorts with dolphin design

swim gloves

swimming cap

nose plug

neoprene socks

one-piece sailor's swimsuit

flippers

robe

diving suit

goggles and snorkel

swimming shorts

inflatable ring

towel

sunglasses

beach hat

beach slippers

artist's apron
with pockets for tools

old T-shirt

artist's shawl

long artist's smock

tubes of paint

headscarf

paper hat

painter's overalls

beret

brushes

mug of water

crayons and pencils

sweatshirt with artist's own design

old denim shirt

torn jeans

colorful sneakers

socks with a fun pattern

artist's palette

easel
with canvas

# WHAT SHOULD
# I WEAR NOW?

Jana Sedláčková
Alexandra Májová

© B4U Publishing for Albatros,
an imprint of Albatros Media Group, 2023
5. května 1746/22, Prague 4, Czech Republic
Written by Jana Sedláčková
Illustrations @ Alexandra Májová
Translated by Andrew Oakland
Edited by Scott Alexander Jones

Printed in China by Leo Paper Group